I Wonder Why

Zippers Have Teeth

and Other Questions About Inventions

Barbara Taylor

Kingfisher

NEW YORK

KINGFISHER
Larousse Kingfisher Chambers Inc.
95 Madison Avenue
New York, New York 10016

First edition 1995
(HC) 10 9 8 7 6 5 4 3 2 1
(RLB) 10 9 8 7 6 5 4 3 2 1

LIBRARY OF CONGRESS CATALOGING-IN PUBLICATION DATA
Taylor, Barbara
I wonder why zippers have teeth and other questions about
inventions (Barbara Taylor, 1st American ed. p. cm.—(I
wonder why)
Includes Index.
Summary: Answers wide variety of questions about the
invention of common household items.
1. Inventions—Miscellanea— Juvenile literature.
(1. Inventions—Miscellanea. 2 Questions and Answers.) 1.
Title. II. Series: I wonder why (New York, N.Y.)
T48.T22 1996
608—dc20 95—25190 CIP AC
ISBN 1-85697-670-X (HC)
ISBN 1-85697-688-2 (RLB)
ISBN 1-85697-691-2 (PB)
Printed in Italy

Series editor: Clare Oliver
Series designer: David West Children's Books
Illustrations: Susanna Addario 28-29; Peter Dennis (Linda
    Rogers) 10-11, 18-19; Chris Forsey cover, 22tl, 26tl,
    30-31; Terry Gabbey (AFA Ltd.) 20-21; Ruby Green
    14-15, 26-27; Nick Harris (Virgil Pomfret) 24-25; Biz
    Hull (Artist Partners) 4-5, 16-17, 22-23; Tony Kenyon
    (B.L. Kearley) all cartoons; Nicki Palin 6-7, 8-9, 12-13.

CONTENTS

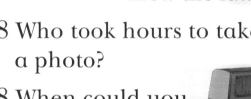

Why do people invent things?

Inventors try to solve problems. They think about people's needs and come up with an answer. When an inventor noticed how inconvenient big umbrellas were, he invented a folding one that would fit in a bag.

Gone to buy some glue!

● Post-it notes were invented by accident when someone made a glue that didn't stick properly. You could stick down a piece of paper, peel it off, and then restick it!

● From the moment you wake up you're surrounded by inventions. Pillows, light bulbs, and even cornflakes all help to give us a more comfortable life.

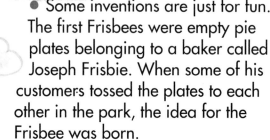

● Some inventions are just for fun. The first Frisbees were empty pie plates belonging to a baker called Joseph Frisbie. When some of his customers tossed the plates to each other in the park, the idea for the Frisbee was born.

Is everything invented?

No it isn't! An invention is something new like a paper clip, which never existed before someone thought of it. But things like coal and rubber weren't invented. They were already in the world and just had to be discovered.

● When people first discovered the milky juice of the rubber tree they used it to make rubber. Later, someone invented rubber tires for cars and bicycles.

Where do inventors get their ideas?

Inventors get ideas for their inventions in lots of different places. Some of them study plants and animals to see how they have solved their problems. Others look at ideas from other places or from the past. Very few ideas come out of the blue.

● Burdock seeds are covered with tiny hooks that stick to things but can be pulled off. An engineer who noticed this used his discovery to make Velcro for fastenings.

Which new invention was soon on everyone's lips?

In 1915 scientists came up with a small invention that was a huge success. It was a creamy stick of color inside a case that could be twisted up and used on the lips—the very first lipstick.

● Ancient Egyptian women didn't have twist-up lipsticks, but they did color their lips. They used golden clay mixed with juicy tree sap.

Who wore a mouthful of hippo teeth?

Around 2,500 years ago people began to make false teeth from ivory or bone. Hippo bone was popular, but so was ox, cat, and human bone. Unfortunately, all these false teeth soon turned brown and started to rot. They must have tasted disgusting!

- Before lipsticks, lip colors came in a pot. Many of them were waxes and ointments colored with plant dyes such as grape juice.

- A French hairdresser has used a video camera linked to a computer to show his clients what they would look like with different styles—short hair, long hair, or no hair at all!

Why were Band-Aids invented?

Earl Dickson invented Band-Aids for his wife, who often cut herself in the kitchen. He stuck small squares of cloth onto pieces of tape, covering them carefully to stop the glue from drying out. Whenever his wife cut herself, she just grabbed a piece of the tape and stuck it on.

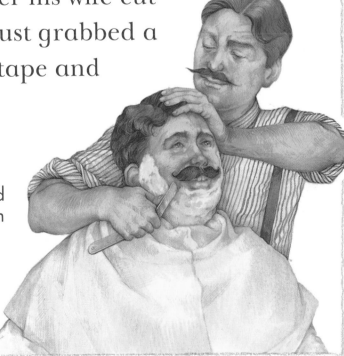

- Before Mr. King Camp Gillette invented safe, modern razors in 1895, men shaved with sharp open razors—and hoped that their hand wouldn't slip!

Who first flushed the toilet?

Four hundred years ago Sir John Harrington built a flushing toilet for his godmother, Queen Elizabeth I. In those days few homes had pipes or drains—most people continued to use chamber pots until the late 1800s.

● The problem with this shower from the 1800s was that you had to pump the water yourself—with your foot. No wonder it never really caught on!

● About 100 years ago, flush toilets were highly-prized pieces of furniture. They were often beautifully decorated with fruit, flowers, animals, or shells.

Who first jumped in the tub?

The people of Greece, Rome, and the Indus Valley in Pakistan all enjoyed a bath in ancient times. But as time went by, baths went out of fashion and many people never even washed. They used perfumes to cover up the smell!

● The Chinese used pig's hair to make the first toothbrushes about 500 years ago. Luckily for pigs, nylon brushes came along in the 1930s!

How did horses help keep carpets clean?

The first carpet-cleaning machine was towed by horses! It was parked outside the house because of its smelly gasoline engine. Long pipes stretched through the windows and sucked up all the dirt. It was quite a sight and people often invited their friends around to watch!

Who invented raincoats?

● A lot of today's rainwear is made of PVC. It's a plastic-backed material which comes in lots of bright colors.

The first waterproof raincoats were made in 1823 by Charles Macintosh. He made the cloth waterproof by sandwiching a layer of rubber between two lengths of cotton. The coats kept people dry all right, but they weighed a ton and smelled awful when they got wet!

● It rains so much in Scotland that farmers sometimes buy raincoats for their sheep!

Why do zippers have teeth?

The two rows of teeth on a zipper are joined by a slider, which locks them together or pulls them apart. Zippers were invented in the 1890s and were a great improvement on tiny buttons and hooks.

● The first jeans were made by Levi Strauss for gold miners in San Francisco. He made them in a hard-wearing blue cloth that was used to make tents. These days it's better known as denim.

Can clothes keep you feeling fit?

Some clothes can do amazing things. You can even buy panty hose full of health-giving vitamins, which are usually found in fresh fruit and vegetables!

● When Thomas Hancock invented elastic in 1820, he thought it would be useful along the top of pockets to stop thieves. It was someone else who realized it would be just right for holding up people's underwear!

What did people use before they had refrigerators?

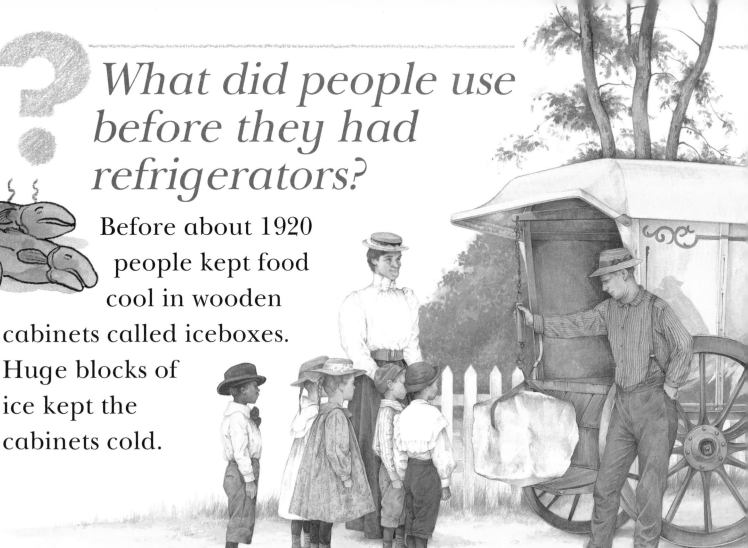

Before about 1920 people kept food cool in wooden cabinets called iceboxes. Huge blocks of ice kept the cabinets cold.

• Coca-Cola didn't start out as a fizzy drink. A pharmacist called John Pemberton invented it as a sweet syrup in 1885. Soda water was added to it later.

Who ate the first cornflakes?

Two brothers, Will and John Kellogg, invented cornflakes by accident when they were trying to make a new type of bread. One day, they overcooked a pan of wheat, rolled the mixture flat, and then watched it dry into flakes. They toasted the flakes and tasted them—delicious!

- The iceman visited several times a week to deliver large blocks of ice for the icebox.

- Long ago, people made natural refrigerators by lining caves and holes with a thick layer of snow in winter. These icehouses kept fresh food cool throughout the warm summer months.

- In 1853, a new food was invented. When a diner asked for extra-thin french fries, the chef came up with the first potato chips.

How were drinking straws invented?

One hot summer in the 1880s, a man called Marvin Stone made the first paper straw. He'd noticed that people kept drinks cooler by not touching the glass and using a hollow grass stalk to suck up the liquid.

Why are bears called teddies?

Teddy bears are named after President Theodore Roosevelt, who was called Teddy for short. Once, on a hunting trip, he came across a bear cub and refused to shoot it. A candy store owner who read the story in the paper decided to give up his store and make toy bears. He called them teddies, after the president.

● The construction toys Lego and Erector were both invented to encourage children to build things, not destroy them! You can use them to make all sorts of inventions!

● Playing cards were invented in Asia more than 1,000 years ago.

Which toy is 6,000 years old?

Dolls are probably the oldest toys of all. Roman children played with dolls made of rags. Dolls have been made from all kinds of materials—wood, wax, paper, china, and plastic.

● Barbie went on sale in 1959. She was the first doll ever to have a grown-up's body.

When did home computer games appear?

The first home computer games appeared in 1974. Compared to today's games, they weren't very exciting. There were no life-and-death battles in outer space—you hit a ball back and forth with a bat!

How do you make toast without a toaster?

People made toast long before there were electric toasters. They put a piece of bread on the end of a long toasting fork and held it in front of a fire. The bread burned easily, though, and needed very careful watching. The first pop-up toaster was invented about 70 years ago.

● Electric toasters save us from having to keep an eye on the toast—and from burning it, too!

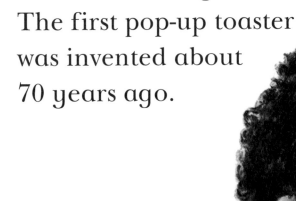

● In 1937 a new automatic tea-making machine was invented. It heated water, made the tea and then woke you with an alarm.

Who invented the microwave oven?

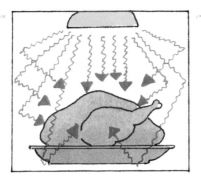

● Microwaves are invisible waves of energy. When they're beamed at food, any water in the food starts to shake violently and gets very hot. The heat passes quickly through the food and cooks it all the way through.

Percy Spencer invented the microwave oven just after World War II. He'd been working on ways of using invisible waves to detect enemy planes. When the waves melted the chocolate bar in his pocket, he realized they'd be useful for cooking too!

● About 100 years ago, only rich people had electricity in their homes. The first electrical gadgets were dangerous things, and servants sometimes risked their lives by using them.

Why don't nonstick frying pans stick?

Nonstick pans don't stick because they are coated with something called Teflon, which is very slippery. Teflon is a kind of plastic and was invented in the late 1930s. It took years for someone to think of sticking the stuff onto pots and pans!

Who scored points in a basket?

The very first basketball players used two old peach baskets as nets. Basketball was invented about 100 years ago by coach James Naismith, who was looking for an exciting game to play indoors on cold winter nights.

Why are sneakers so springy?

Sneakers have springy soles made of rubber and little pockets of air. Each time you take a step, the rubber gets squashed down, but quickly springs back to its original size. All this squashing and springing makes your feet bounce off the ground and helps you to run a little bit faster.

● Roller-skating was all the rage in the late 1800s. At the ballet in Paris, ballerinas even danced in them!

● Early basketball players had to climb a ladder to get the ball back after a basket. Things are easier today—now the nets have a hole in the bottom.

How did people ice-skate in summer?

Before there were ice rinks, people could only ice-skate outdoors in the winter. Then someone came up with the idea of making a "ground" skate that people could enjoy in the summer, too. Instead of a blade, they put wheels on the sole and abracadabra—the roller skate had arrived!

● Jet-skis first went on sale in Japan in 1979. Jet-skiers have to steer well clear of swimmers. The very latest models can zoom along at speeds of 65 mph.

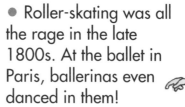

What were the first cars like?

The first cars were steam engines on wheels—noisy, smoky machines that scared other road-users! But these steam cars soon became quicker and easier to drive. They were used for nearly 30 years, until they were replaced by faster cars with gasoline engines.

- In the 1930s, planes carried 20 passengers at the most. By the 1970s, the new jumbo jets could seat up to 500! Soon, new super-jumbos will carry as many as 850 people!

How do you ride on air?

People ride on air every time they travel on a hovercraft. The hovercraft was invented by Christopher Cockerell in 1959. He discovered that trapping a cushion of air beneath a boat lifts it up above the waves, allowing it to travel much faster.

• The high-wheeler bicycle was invented in the 1860s. It had two wheels—one very large and one very small.

• Eveyone knows about seat belts for people to wear, but did you know that cats and dogs can wear them too? So buckle up, Rover and Felix!

Which bikes have sails?

• The first cars weren't allowed to go faster than 2 mph. And someone had to walk in front with a flag to warn other road-users!

The fastest superbikes have solid wheels and flat frames that work in the same way as a sail. As the bike zooms along, its wheels and frame catch the wind, which helps to push the bike forward— just as a sail does on a boat. But most of the power still comes from turning the pedals!

How can you fit 1,000 books in your pocket?

There's room for around 1,000 storybooks on a CD-ROM—a small compact disc that's as thin as your fingernail and can fit in a pocket. Words, pictures, and sounds can all be stored on CD-ROMs, but they only work with a computer, so you can't read one on the bus—yet!

● The Egyptians were one of the first peoples to write with ink. They made it by mixing black soot with sticky tree sap.

● Just like dinosaurs, the typewriter will soon be extinct. It was a new invention in 1873 but has now been replaced by computers and word processors.

● Felt-tip pens went on sale in Japan in 1962. Their inventor hoped that the pen's soft tip would make people's handwriting more graceful—like the brushstrokes in Japanese writing.

● Today's pocket calculators can carry out calculations much quicker than you can move your fingers. They are as powerful as the huge computers of the 1960s.

Which computer was as big as a bus?

The first computer was about as long as four buses and was called Colossus. It was built in Britain and was switched on in 1943. Very few people knew about it at the time, because one of its first jobs was to crack secret codes during World War II.

Who was Mr. Biro?

Ladislao Biro invented a ballpoint pen in 1938. It contained a tube of long-lasting, quick-drying ink, which rolled evenly onto the paper thanks to a tiny ball at the tip. Biro called his pen a ballpoint, but in many countries ballpoints are still called biros!

How did a cash register settle an argument?

In James Ritty's saloon in Ohio, customers were always arguing with the staff about how much they had to pay for their drinks. So in 1879 Ritty invented a cash register, which rang up prices, kept a record of how much money had been taken in, and gave Ritty and his staff more peace!

● Since 1980, goods sold in stores have had a bar code on them. Only a laser scanner can understand the bar code's pattern, which contains all kinds of information about the item.

Who used tea as money?

People in Tibet and China once used tea pressed into blocks as money. Before coins were invented, people used to trade things like shells, beads, or grain for the goods they wanted.

● The Chinese first used paper money about 1,200 years ago. They printed some of their bills on the bark of the mulberry tree.

How can a shopping cart make you rich?

The person who invented the world's first supermarket shopping cart became a millionaire. Sylvan Goldman's cart was little more than a chair on wheels with two baskets on top, but it earned him a fortune.

● Inventions don't have to be grand. When Margaret Knight invented flat-bottomed paper bags, she became a wealthy woman. The bags held twice as much shopping!

Which came first—screws or screwdrivers?

● Today's carpenters use many of the same tools as carpenters long ago.

Spiral or twisted nails were used in the 1500s in guns, armor, and clocks. But strangely, you couldn't unscrew a screw for another 300 years—when the handy screwdriver first appeared.

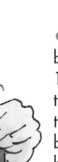

● Screws weren't made by machine until the 1760s. Before then the thread that runs around the screw had to be filed by hand. That must have been a difficult task!

Who had everything under lock and key?

The ancient Egyptians invented locks. Two wooden bolts fitted together snugly and were held in place by pins arranged in a pattern. The pins could only be freed with a key that had a matching pattern.

• With growing bags you can grow plants anywhere—even if you don't have a yard. These bags of earth first appeared in 1973.

Could a horse mow the lawn?

The first lawn mowers were pulled by horses. The animals had to wear big rubber boots so they didn't leave messy hoof-prints all over the freshly-mowed lawn!

• Lawn mower engines were used on the first go-karts. Today's Grand Prix champions probably all started out driving lawn mowers!

Who took hours to take a photo?

A Frenchman called Joseph Niépce took the first photograph in 1826. He had to wait eight hours before the picture was captured on a thin metal plate coated with a sort of tar. The photo was of the view from his window.

● In the late 1800s, it took so long to take a photo that sitters needed a backrest to help them sit still!

● Niépce would have found it hard to believe, but today's Polaroid cameras can produce a picture in seconds!

When could you watch pink TV?

The first TV had an odd picture —bright pink and very fuzzy! But its inventor, John Logie Baird, had used very odd equipment to build it, including a bicycle light and a knitting needle!

The world's smallest radio is about the size of a pea!

Who invented the personal stereo?

A Walkman is a personal cassette player with headphones that is light enough to carry around. It was invented in 1979 by a Japanese electrical company called Sony.

• The first telephone service started in 1878, in New Haven, Connecticut. Only 20 people had phones, so they could only call each other!

How can you fight a hungry dinosaur?

When you put on a virtual reality helmet, you enter an imaginary world. You could be fighting a man-eating dinosaur or visiting aliens in space. Everything inside the helmet looks and sounds real but is actually created by a computer.

● As you press buttons in the special data-glove, the computer changes the pictures you see and the sounds you hear.

● Anyone can be an inventor! What would you like to invent?

● Scientists are experimenting with fruit and vegetables to produce useful, tasty foods. One day they may come up with square tomatoes that you can stack neatly on a shelf.

Are there insects on Mars?

No, but there soon will be! Scientists are building small robots to explore Mars and other planets. The robots have six legs, and look like giant insects. They appear to behave like insects too, because they've been programed to look for food. The food's not for them, though—it's for us, if we ever live on Mars!

● Cars of the future may have a computer on board, which could plan the driver's route. It would even warn drivers of traffic jams on the road ahead and suggest a good shortcut.

Index